W9-BFC-780

10/11

MYSTERY EXPLORERS™

SEARCHING FOR

UFOS

rosen publishing's
rosen
central

New York

Dillon H. Richards
and Janet I. Stirling

Published in 2012 by The Rosen Publishing Group, Inc.
29 East 21st Street, New York, NY 10010

First Edition

Library of Congress Cataloging-in-Publication Data

Richards, Dillon H.
Searching for UFOS/Dillon H. Richards, Janet I. Stirling.—1st ed.
       p. cm.—(Mystery explorers)
Includes bibliographical references and index.
ISBN 978-1-4488-4765-5 (library binding)—
ISBN 978-1-4488-4766-2 (pbk.)—
ISBN 978-1-4488-4774-7 (6-pack)
1. Unidentified flying objects—Juvenile literature. I. Stirling, Janet. II. Title.
TL789.2.R53 2012
001.942—dc22

                                                                      2011006511

Manufactured in the United States of America

CPSIA Compliance Information: Batch #S11YA: For further information, contact Rosen Publishing, New York, New York, at 1-800-237-9932.

CONTENTS

INTRODUCTION

What do you think of when you hear the term "UFO"? Do you think of the adorable candy fiend *E.T.: The Extra Terrestrial* visiting Earth in the 1980s? Or do you imagine the human-looking aliens with dark intentions like on the television series *V*? Or do you simply imagine a mysterious disc streaking across the sky while a curious bystander frantically tries to snap a picture before the moment is gone?

The phrase "unidentified flying object" by itself isn't actually very exciting—until you consider what it means to most of us. When the average person hears someone say "UFO," he or she doesn't think of lost weather balloons or unusually high-flying eagles. What unidentified flying object means to the average person is spaceships, aliens, and the possibility that our planet is being watched by beings of higher intelligence, or at least more advanced technology, even though the term is actually used to describe any flying object that cannot easily be identified.

Some people even think that UFOs are visitors from the distant future, or that they might be some species of unknown animal. For the last few hundred years, the idea of intelligent life on other planets has spawned multiple books, movies, and TV shows and gained a following of "believers." How much of it is real?

A good question to ask ourselves about UFOs and extraterrestrial life might be: Is all of this even possible? Or is there such a thing as being too skeptical?

We've gathered together some reports about UFOs that might help you make up your own mind. We will also discuss the alien phenomenon as a part of pop culture that has spawned much of science fiction from low-budget to blockbuster films and from the small screen to the big screen.

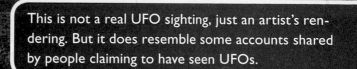

This is not a real UFO sighting, just an artist's rendering. But it does resemble some accounts shared
by people claiming to have seen UFOs.

CHAPTER 1

The First Sightings

How long have people been seeing strange things in the sky? Probably since there have been people to notice that something up there was different.

How long have people been assuming that those strange things were manufactured objects? At least since the late nineteenth century.

Between November 1896 and April 1897, there was a rash of sightings of a mysterious "airship" (which describes the most advanced flying technology of the time) whose origins, purpose, and crew were unknown. People described it as having a cylindrical gasbag with wings and propellers.

Aurora, Texas

On April 19, 1897, the *Dallas Morning News* published a report of such an airship allegedly crashing in the town of Aurora in Wise County, Texas.

This UFO enthusiast in Aurora, Texas, checks the sky for signs of anything mysterious. Green skin and large, luminous eyes, like the ones on the mask worn here, fit the description of many alien sightings.

According to the article, it collided with the tower of a windmill and exploded, scattering debris over several acres.

To quote the article, "The pilot of the ship is assumed to have been the only one aboard, and while his remains are badly disfigured, enough of the original has been picked up to show that he was not an inhabitant of this world." The article then goes on to give the time of the "pilot's" funeral.

This incident was forgotten until the late 1960s, when an article in the *Flying Saucer Review* attracted investigators to Aurora. They found that no windmill had ever existed in the spot the article indicated and that there were no unmarked graves in the local cemetery.

In 1973, another article claimed that elderly citizens of the town remembered the crash and had even collected "unidentified" metal from it. It also claimed that the UFO pilot's grave had been found through the use of a metal detector and that a "unique handmade headstone" was found on the spot. A court order was sought to exhume the "spaceman's" body.

Then, on July 4, 1973, the *Dallas Times Herald* carried the headline, "Grave Believed UFO Pilot's At Aurora, Entered, Robbed."

Once again investigation proved that things were not as they seemed. The hand carved "tombstone" was a scarred rock, and the old-timers who had been interviewed all said they'd been misquoted and had never said they recalled the incident.

In the end, there was not one shred of evidence to back up the story of the Aurora crash.

Sightings During Wartime

Then, between 1909 and 1919, "airships" were seen over England. They were believed to be Germans, not aliens, scouting for an invasion. Reports of sightings also came in from Europe, the United States, Canada, Japan, New Zealand, and South Africa, possibly the result of nervousness about World War I.

From 1909 until his death in 1932, Charles Fort, a well-known writer about strange occurrences, reported numerous incidents of "unknown, luminous things" seen in the sky, many of them disk-shaped.

American writer Charles Fort spent much of his adult life at the New York Public Library going through newspapers in search of stories about anything mysterious or unexplained.

MARACAIBO, VENEZUELA

On October 24, 1886, the nine members of a family in Maracaibo, Venezuela, were sound asleep when suddenly they were awakened by dazzling lights and a strange humming noise outside their house. Terrified, the people fell to their knees and began to pray, but this was soon interrupted by bouts of violent vomiting and swelling in the upper body, particularly around their faces and lips. The next morning the lights were gone as was the swelling, but in its place the people found black blotches all over their bodies. Nine days later, the skin peeled away around the blotches and left red, raw sores in their place. The people began to lose their hair. Doctors found that the symptoms were very similar to those of radiation poisoning, but the house itself had suffered no damage, and throughout the event, none of the windows or doors had been open. It should also be noted that on the ninth day after the incident, all of the trees surrounding the house withered and died.

The story of the family appeared later that year in an article in *Scientific American*. To this day, their incident remains a mystery.

Then, just before and during World War II, there were reports of ghost planes in the skies over Europe. Allied pilots often reported seeing what they dubbed "Foo-Fighters" accompanying their flights. The objects were described as "large orange glows" or "small amber disks."

At first these were feared to be a Nazi secret weapon, but they appeared in the Pacific as well. None were reported to have directly interfered with Allied planes or crews—they simply flew quietly alongside them. After a while less was heard of these objects, until they became an occasionally told UFO/ghost story.

Ghost Rockets

After the war, beginning in May 1946, Sweden experienced sightings of spool-, torpedo-, or cigar-shaped rocketlike objects, often with small fins attached. At the time the fear was that German rocket technology was being used by the Soviets, and an extraterrestrial origin wasn't suspected. Between May and December, 997 sightings were reported. Over two hundred were of the "rocket-shaped" variety and were described as "metallic."

Soon other nations began to make reports of "ghost rockets." France, Denmark, Norway, Spain, Greece, Morocco, Portugal, and Turkey viewed flashing lights in their skies, sometimes accompanied by "an infernal roaring." Eventually the Swedes were able to identify 80 percent of their sightings. The rest were listed as unidentified.

CHAPTER 2

Twentieth-Century Sightings

On June 24, 1947, Kenneth Arnold, a successful businessman and private pilot, was on his way home and intended to make a detour to Yakima, Washington, to help search for a missing troop transport.

It was about three o'clock in the afternoon; he was flying at 9,200 feet (2,804 meters), and the air was crystal clear—excellent flying weather. A flash of light off to the left caught his eye, and he looked toward Mount Ranier. He described what he saw as "a chain of nine peculiar looking aircraft flying from north to south at approximately 9,500 feet (2,896 m) elevation and going, seemingly, in a definite direction of about 170 degrees." Arnold estimated that they were between 20 and 25 miles (32 to 40 kilometers) away.

They were flying at a high rate of speed and were bobbing and weaving slightly, which caused them to flash in the sunlight. Arnold timed them as they passed Mount Rainier in the direction of Mount Adams. It took 102 seconds for the objects to pass between the two peaks. It is 47 miles (76 km) between Mounts Ranier and Adams, which gives the objects a ground speed of 1,700 miles per hour (2,735 km per hour). The speed of sound is approximately 740 mph (1,191 km per hour), making the mysterious objects capable of flying at over twice the speed of sound! In 1947, no aircraft on Earth had that capability.

When Arnold later drew a picture of the crafts, he showed them having a flattened teardrop shape with a curved front surface, straight sides, and a back end with a rounded point. They were about 50 feet long (15 m), he thought, a bit less wide, but only 3 feet (1 m) thick. They had a mirror finish.

Arnold took his maps and calculations to the local FBI office but found it closed. He then went to the *East Oregonian* newspaper and spoke to an editor there. The report that went out on the Associated Press wire said that "nine bright, saucer-like objects flying at 'incredible speed' at 10,000 feet altitude were reported here today."

Most researchers agree that this is the sighting that gave us the term "flying saucers."

A High-Altitude Sighting

Captain Thomas Mantell was an experienced pilot who flew with the Kentucky Air National Guard 165th Fighter Squadron. His plane, an F-51 Mustang, was

Kenneth Arnold spotted a formation of bright lights while flying over the Cascade Mountains in Washington state. His description of the sighting coined the term "flying saucer."

propeller driven, with a top speed of 437 mph (703 kph) and a ceiling of 41,900 feet (12,771 m), which could only be reached if the plane carried oxygen.

On January 7, 1948, none of the planes in Captain Mantell's squadron had oxygen because their mission was a low-altitude training flight.

At about 1:20 PM, the Kentucky State Police reported to the Fort Knox base that "an unusual aircraft or object . . . circular in appearance, approximately 250–300 feet (76–91 m) in diameter" had been seen over Mansville, Kentucky. Fort Knox alerted Godman Airforce Base (AFB), which sighted the object at 1:45 PM. It looked roughly like a parachute with a red light at the bottom and was whiter than the clouds around it. It appeared to be either stationary or moving very slowly. Witness PFC Stanley Oliver said, "[T]o me it had the resemblance of an ice cream cone topped with red." It was much too large for any known balloon.

Civilians saw it, too, and reports came in from towns separated by as much as 175 miles (282 km). This means that the object must have been from 25 to 50 miles (40–80 km) high. At that time the United States had no plane that could fly so high.

At approximately 2:40 PM, Captain Mantell's group of four F-51s turned toward the object and began a spiral climb. At 2:45 Mantell reported, "The object is directly ahead of me and above me now, moving at about half my speed. It appears to be a metallic object, or possibly reflection of sun from a metallic object, and it is of tremendous size." At about 3:15 he reported, "I'm still climbing, the object is above and ahead of me moving at about my speed or faster. I'm trying to close in for a better look."

Somewhere between 15,000 and 22,000 feet (4,572–6,706 m), the other pilots turned back due to lack of oxygen. Mantell told the tower that he would go to 25,000 feet (7,620 m) for ten minutes. There followed a few garbled transmissions and then silence. Both radio and visual contact with Mantell had been lost. At 3:50 PM, the Godman tower lost sight of the object.

It was seen by others and described as "huge, fluid. It had a metallic sheen and looked like an upside-down ice cream cone." At approximately 4:45 PM, an astronomer at Vanderbilt University watched an object in the sky south-east of Nashville, Tennessee, and described it as "a pear-shaped balloon with cables and a basket attached." Just before sunset, a number of airfield towers reported a flaming object in the midwestern sky, where it was visible for twenty minutes and then sank below the horizon.

A little after 5:00 PM, the shattered remains of Captain Mantell's F-51 were found on a farm in Franklin, Kentucky. The Captain's watch had stopped at 3:18, probably the time when his plane struck the earth.

There have been a lot of dramatic stories about Captain Mantell: that his body was missing from the crashed plane, or that he bore strange wounds. According to records neither claim is true.

The simple truth appears to be that his curiosity got the better of him and he climbed so high that he blacked out from lack of oxygen, and his plane went into a spin and crashed.

The Air Force stated that Captain Mantell had been chasing a combination of the planet Venus and two balloons, and then closed the case.

In 1952, an investigator for Project Bluebook, the Air Force's famous study of UFOs, reopened the Mantell case. The investigator, Captain Edward J. Ruppelt, knew about the Navy's high-altitude research, classified in 1948, that used the huge Skyhook balloons. These balloons are 100 feet (30 m) tall and 70 feet (21 m) in diameter—as large as a small apartment building. He tried to discover a launch date that might have put one of the balloons in the vicinity of Mantell's flight.

But Captain Ruppelt could not verify that a Skyhook balloon had been released that day. As for Venus, while it had been seen in the daytime on that particular day, it could hardly be described as "enormous."

What could have distracted an experienced pilot to the extent that he ignored the dangers of oxygen deprivation and continued to pursue this UFO to his death?

Sighting in the Sky

At around 9:00 PM on October 1, 1948, George F. Gorman of the North Dakota Air National Guard claimed to have an actual "dogfight" with a UFO.

He had remained in the air to do some night flying after the rest of his squadron had landed. The air was clear and there was no moon. His speed was 270 mph (435 km per hour) at an altitude of 1,500 feet (457 m). Below him he could see a Piper Cub circling a football field. All was peaceful.

Then he noticed a blinking light moving swiftly from east to west. He contacted the air base's tower to see if there were other aircraft nearby. The answer was no. The pilot of the Piper Cub confirmed that he could see both the F-51 and the blinking light.

Gorman sped off at full power to investigate. The object was traveling too fast to be caught by flying straight after it, so he turned in an attempt to cut it off. The light circled to the left, so Gorman circled to the right intending to confront it head-on. As it approached him a collision seemed unavoidable, but the object veered off and passed over Gorman's plane.

"It was a ball of light, 6 to 8 inches (15–20 cm) in diameter," he said later. "When it began flying at high speed the light increased in intensity and stopped flashing."

Flying at high altitudes, Captain Thomas Mantell crashed while in pursuit of a mysterious object in the sky. Was the object a sign of alien life?

For a moment the lieutenant lost sight of the object, only to find that it had made a turn and was heading straight for him. Suddenly it began to climb. He pushed his F-51 after it, but at 14,000 feet (4,267 m) his plane stalled out. He recovered and again began circling toward the light. It pulled away and again headed straight toward him. He managed to get above the object at 14,000 feet (4,267 m) and went to full power, hoping to catch it as he dove. The light began to climb as though it would make another head-on pass, but instead went vertical and continued to climb until it was out of sight.

Later Gorman said, "I am convinced that there was definite thought behind its maneuvers."

Gorman's F-51 was checked with a Geiger counter and the reading showed measurably more radioactivity than nearby planes that hadn't been flown. Further investigation ruled out other aircraft or weather balloons in the area. This radioactivity seemed to be the first real evidence of an encounter with a flying saucer.

But by 1948 the case began to fall apart. The radioactivity was found to be typical for an aircraft flying at over 20,000 feet (6,096 m), where the thinner atmosphere offers less protection from cosmic rays that show up as increased radioactivity.

In fact, a lighted weather balloon was in the area at the time of the "dogfight." The fancy flying the light seemed to be performing was an illusion caused by its movement, Gorman's own enthusiastic flying, and the lack of a reference point in the night sky. Furthermore, the witnesses in the Piper Cub didn't describe the light moving in the way Gorman said it did.

In 1949, Sidney Shalett, a writer with the *Saturday Evening Post*, located in Indiana, asked a pilot to make several passes at a weather balloon to see if it would appear to be a highly maneuverable, pilot-operated flying saucer.

Shalett reported, "He came down and told me, with some surprise, it definitely appeared to be turning at the same rate as his plane, and at times it even seemed to be turning faster than his aircraft."

On October 13, 2010, several New Yorkers were stopped in their tracks by the appearance of "clusters of shiny round objects" floating over the city. The sighting prompted several calls to 911; some people even claimed that the objects seemed to light up and flash. Almost immediately, videos of the incident went up on the Internet, prompting interest all over the world.

However, the excitement died down pretty quickly when some school kids from nearby Westchester who had been planning a big engagement party for their teacher admitted that some of their balloons had flown away and were likely the cause of the "sighting."

All of this would seem to completely discredit Second Lieutenant Gorman's experience.

Except Gorman had never claimed to fly to 20,000 feet (6,096 m).

The Kinross Disappearance

This case is called the Kinross Disappearance after the Air Force base from which Lieutenant Felix Moncla Jr.'s F-89 jet interceptor scrambled.

On November 23, 1953, Truax AFB picked up a radar blip in a restricted airspace. As a precaution, Moncla and his radar officer R. R. Wilson were sent to investigate.

Many UFO sightings can be attributed to weather balloons. This type of balloon can rise to high altitudes and may be seen from passing aircraft by people on the ground.

The object had been holding still, but suddenly it flashed off across Lake Superior while remaining visible on ground radar.

Lieutenant Moncla raced after the object at over 500 miles per hour (805 km per hour). After nine minutes, the F-89 began to gain slightly on the object. Ground radar operators watched as the jet closed in on the unidentified blip, until the blips suddenly seemed to merge into one.

The operators weren't alarmed at first, because there was no way to tell how high either of the blips was flying. It was assumed that Moncla had flown over or under the UFO. But the single blip simply stayed there for a moment, then flashed off the screen.

Lieutenant Felix Moncla spotted a strange object hovering over Lake Superior. An aerial view of the lake is shown here. Moncla and his radar officer disappeared without a trace while trying to investigate the sighting.

All efforts to contact Moncla by radio failed. Search and rescue crews combed the area for hours aided by the Canadian Air Force. They found nothing: no trace of wreckage, no oil slick, no bodies. The *Chicago Tribune* stated that the radar operator claimed the plane had hit something.

The United States Air Force quickly denied this. After suggesting that the F-89 might have hit a Canadian DC-3 or an RCAF jet, the Canadian Air Force denied that any of its aircraft were over the lake during the chase.

It's possible that the F-89 dropped into the lake without breaking up, in which case the usual signs of a crash wouldn't be apparent. That doesn't explain why radio contact ceased, or why Moncla and Wilson didn't eject. And there have been numerous reports of radio transmissions being interfered with and automobile engines being stopped by UFOs.

Shortly after this incident, two fighter pilots reported that they were being followed by a UFO. Before signaling the base, they went through a series of maneuvers to make sure they weren't seeing a reflection on their canopies or perhaps an unusually bright planet. But the large, bright object stayed in the same position and continued following them. After what had happened to Moncla they were understandably reluctant to turn in pursuit. Finally, as they neared the base, the pilots decided to make their move and turned toward the UFO.

For a split second it continued to follow, then flashed off at high speed. In both cases the pursued object was never satisfactorily identified.

In 1962, a UFO was detected by radar over the Oneida, New York, area, heading west at a high altitude. As the object moved into the Midwest, the Air Defense Command began alerting bases to watch for it. In Phoenix, Arizona, interceptors were scrambled to seek it out. In Utah, witnesses who saw the bright, oval-shaped, red-orange object flash overhead claimed to hear a sound like jet engines. This is unusual, because UFOs are mostly described as soundless or emitting a slight whine.

The UFO was sighted near Eureka, Utah, where it touched down briefly. It was thought to have interrupted electrical service from a nearby power station. A few minutes later it was seen heading west again. Suddenly, 70 miles (113 km) northeast of Las Vegas, the object disappeared from radar screens at a time and place that coincided with reports of a blinding midair explosion.

On April 19, the *Las Vegas Sun* ran a headline stating, "Brilliant Red Explosion Flares in Las Vegas Sky." The roar of the explosion was heard for miles and the flash of light was so brilliant that it lit up the town of Reno like the noonday sun. Police searched the desert for wreckage but found nothing.

Project Bluebook listed it as a radar case, confirming that it had been traced by radar. However, the report stated that there was insufficient information for a scientific analysis. The sighting in Eureka had been a meteor, it said.

But meteors can't be tracked by radar, and they don't take off again once they've landed. As for the exploding object over Las Vegas, the Air Force wouldn't label it a meteor and there were no reports of missing aircraft.

Sighting on the Border

In December 1950, a woman visiting a dude ranch in Texas wrote to her husband about a most unusual incident. She and the other guests and ranch workers had observed what seemed to be an airplane in distress flying over-head. They thought it might have come down over the Mexican-American border. The next day several of the ranch cowboys rode out to see if they could find something.

They found wreckage, but it didn't look like any airplane they'd ever seen. There were bodies strewn about, badly burned. The cowboys said it looked as though the craft had been piloted by children.

On April 19, 1962, the sky over Las Vegas was filled with brilliant red explosions. Many have attributed them to UFO phenomena.

The next day they returned to find the area swarming with Mexican and American officials and military personnel arguing over jurisdiction. No one could agree if the crash remains came from north or south of the border. The cowboys were chased off before they could get too close.

The incident was described in a briefing paper for President Dwight Eisenhower. Nothing more is known about it.

Sighting in Brazil

In September 1957, several Brazilian fishermen claimed they had seen a flying disc. It came toward them at a very high speed, dived at them, turned in a tight circle, and began a rapid climb. Seconds later it exploded, showering the beach at Ubatuba with fragments. The men wrote to the local newspaper and included several of the fragments with their letter.

When Dr. Olavo Fontes, the Brazilian representative for the Aerial Phenomena Research Organization (APRO), first read the story, he thought it must be a hoax. But he had the samples of the metal examined by a local chemist. The chemist concluded that it wasn't from a meteorite because it was too light. Many meteors are composed of nickel and iron. But the samples were metal and had been burned.

Spectroscopic analysis revealed that the sample was magnesium and of a purity unobtainable in nature. Dr. Fontes sent a report and the samples to APRO headquarters in the United States.

APRO sent a small piece of the metal to the Air Force for analysis. Unfortunately, their spectrograph operator destroyed the sample without getting an exposed plate. It may have been carelessness or a malfunction, but the destruction of the sample isn't necessarily proof of malice on the part of the Air Force.

APRO then sent a sample to the Atomic Energy Commission, which found that the sample was slightly denser than normal. Lab results also showed that the metal probably came from something that had broken apart rapidly, as in an explosion.

The fragments recovered from a crash site in Brazil were discovered to contain high levels of strontium, a silvery-white element. Strontium can also be found in Celestine, the mineral shown here.

Subsequent analysis by Dr. R. S. Busk of the Condon, Colorado, UFO study revealed a high content of strontium, a soft, silver-white element. The study also said that magnesium of the same purity was created at Dow Laboratories.

It was also found that the Ubatuba samples had better high-temperature properties than samples of the Dow Labs metal. Therefore, although Dow had magnesium of equal purity, it could not have produced the samples from Brazil.

How something only available in an American laboratory came to be found on a beach in Brazil was not something the Condon, Colorado, UFO study commented on.

The Roswell Incident

This has to be the most famous UFO crash ever. Many books have been written about it, so we'll give just the basic story.

On July 2, 1947, many people in Roswell reported a large, disc-shaped object flashing by overhead and showing signs of instability in its flight. An explosion was heard, but because there was a thunderstorm in progress, no particular attention was paid to the burst of sound.

The next morning, objects that were described as everything from scattered debris to "a crashed airplane without wings" or "narrow wings" and "a fat fuselage" were found.

Rancher William "Mac" Brazel found debris scattered over an area nearly 1 mile (1.6 km) long and half a mile (.8 km) wide. He collected some of it and stored it in his barn. Brazel called the sheriff when he heard about the UFO sighting, and soon news about the debris made its way to Major Jesse Marcel at the Roswell Army Air Field.

Marcel visited Brazel's place and collected some samples. Upon Marcel's return to the base, Colonel William Blanchard ordered Lieutenant William Haut to release a statement to the media that the wreckage of a flying disc

This alien is not the real thing, just a model. But many conspiracy theorists believe that alien bodies were recovered from the Roswell crash site. Is there any truth to those claims?

had been recovered. Almost immediately Blanchard's commanders ordered that the story be retracted.

According to Marcel, the samples he recovered included a metal that couldn't be burned but was as light as balsa wood. Some of it appeared to be struts or beams that had hieroglyphic-like writing on them. Hammering on the metal with a hammer produced no dents. There was also a type of foil-like metal that could be crumpled into a ball and then would straighten itself out.

As well-known as the Roswell crash is for

the unique properties of the debris, it's better known for the five alien bodies allegedly found at the site. The bodies were clothed in flight suits without visible fasteners. Each was 5 feet (1.5 m) tall or less, thin and pale, with a head slightly larger than a human's would be, and completely hairless. The aliens' eyes were only slightly larger than those of normal humans and had pupils. Their noses were small but defined and their mouths were lipless. Their hands had four long, thin fingers.

Immediately after the crash, the debris and alleged bodies were spirited away by the Army Air Force (as it was known in 1947) and never seen again.

The most recent press release from the Air Force regarding the Roswell incident claims that a balloon research project code named Mogul crashed in the area. The bodies, it explained, were test dummies born aloft for scientific testing. The Army Air Force units that gathered the material were simply on-site for a normal retrieval.

The Air Force claimed that a number of different incidents, often separated by years, "have been consolidated and represented to have taken place in two or three days in July 1947."

This may be true, but their test dummies, while hairless, have very prominent noses and lips and look much more like puppets than anything that might once have been alive.

CHAPTER 4

Sightings in Space

Several times during their flights, astronauts have seen objects that couldn't be identified. NASA generally knows what's orbiting the earth by keeping track of satellites and space debris such as discarded boosters. So when an astronaut asks about something he or she sees, NASA can usually give a straight answer. But not always.

Astronaut James McDivitt on *Gemini IV* in 1965 spied a silvery-white cylindrical object with arms or antennae projecting from it. It appeared to be moving toward him when suddenly it disappeared.

During an air-to-ground transmission, McDivitt was asked, "You still looking at that thing up there?"

The astronaut answered, "No, I've lost it . . . I only had it for just a minute. I got a couple of pictures . . . but I was in free drift, and before I could get the control back I drifted and lost it."

Astronaut James McDivitt spied a strange object in space while aboard the *Gemini IV*. Here he prepares for that fateful mission. Strange incidents followed with the Gemini V mission.

On the third day of Gemini V, an eight-day mission flown by LeRoy Gordon Cooper and Charles Conrad in August 1965, Flight Director D. Christopher Kraft asked, "Hey, do you guys have anything flying alongside of you?"

The astronauts replied, "Negative. Why did you ask?"

"We have a radar image of a space object going right along with you from two thousand to ten thousand yards (1,829–9,144 m) away," Kraft said. "Their radar return is approximately the same magnitude as Gemini V."

Cooper and Conrad still denied seeing anything.

In the log is the following statement: "A tumbling radar signature was observed. This info is to be withheld pending further investigation."

Cape Canaveral continued to track the UFO until Gemini V dropped below the curve of the earth. When Gemini V reached the next tracking station in Carnarvon, Australia, the UFO was gone.

In 1965, Gemini VII astronauts Frank Borman and James Lowell contacted Houston to say they had "a bogey at twelve o'clock high." Ground control thought at first that it was the booster from their own rocket, but the astronauts said that they had that in sight at the same time as they were watching the UFO. It slowly tumbled out of sight and still remains unidentified.

Michael Collins and John W. Young in Gemini X observed five objects in orbit together. These, too, remain unidentified.

On their way to the first moon landing in 1969, the Apollo XI crew—Aldrin, Armstrong, and Collins—were one day out when they saw something strange. Thinking they were looking at their own Saturn IV booster rocket, they called Houston for confirmation only to be told the booster was 6,000 miles (9,656 km) away.

Shown here after the *Apollo XI* crew landed safely on the moon, Buzz Aldrin was one of the three astronauts to spot a strange object in space before the landing that would launch them into history.

The UFO seemed to the astronauts to be of "a sizeable dimension" and appeared brighter than other objects going by. Armstrong said during the mission debriefing, "We should say it was right at the limit of the resolution of

Ever see an unexplained glowing object in the sky and think it was a UFO? There might be a simple explanation that would have made no sense 100 years ago. Ever since humans have begun to explore space, they've been leaving traces of their travels behind. There are spent rocket stages, dead satellites, and explosion and collision fragments all left by space exploration traveling in orbit around the earth.

If a piece of "space junk" breaks through the atmosphere and falls to Earth, the velocity at which it travels would cause it to burn up, emitting a glow. Could many sightings over the last century be caused by space debris?

the eye. It was very difficult to tell just what shape it was. And there was no way to tell the size without knowing the range [distance from the *Apollo XI*] or the range without knowing the size."

At one angle, the object had a shape something like "an open suitcase." When looked at through an off-focus sextant it appeared "to be a hollow cylinder" or "two rings." When they changed the focus on the sextant, the cylinder was replaced by "this open book shape." The object remains unidentified.

The crew of Skylab II in 1973 also sighted something mysterious in space. It seemed to be a large, star-shaped object, but brighter than a planet or a star. The crew watched it slowly rotate for about ten minutes, estimating that

Dr. Owen K. Garriott was part of the Skylab crew that witnessed a strange rotating object in space in 1973.

it was between 30 and 50 nautical miles (56–93 km) from Sky Lab. Despite the best efforts of NASA and the North American Air Defense Command, it, too, remains unidentified.

CHAPTER 5

Modern Sightings

There seem to be fewer reports these days, but by no means are UFOs finished with us.

Luis Delgado

It was 3:50 AM when Luis Delgado, a patrolman for the Haines City, Florida, police department, caught sight of a green light in his rearview mirror. As he drove, the light seemed to be pacing his cruiser. He slowed down and the object flew over the cruiser with a brilliant green glow. Alarmed, he pulled to a stop and the cruiser's power died, leaving him without a radio.

Delgado stepped out of the car and watched the glowing, 15-foot-wide (4.6 m) object silently hovering about 10 feet (3 m) off the ground in front of him. It cooled the warm night air enough to form a mist around it.

Then, after several minutes, it suddenly sped away.

The young officer returned to his cruiser and found the electrical system working again.

Many times when people out driving see a UFO they report that their cars mysteriously stop. Those with CBs report that their radios won't work either. That makes the above story something of a classic.

Strange Camping Trip

Four friends had gathered in the wilds of central Idaho for their annual hunt, as they'd been doing for over twenty years, when they saw something very strange.

It was almost 10 PM when one of them left their camper to get some food from his pickup truck. He suddenly felt strange, "like a thick blanket was suspended overhead." As he stepped up on the rear tire of his truck to reach the food, his flashlight beam swung upward and illuminated something directly above him. Glancing up, he was so startled that he fell from the truck to his knees in shock.

Silent and dark, the object hung motionless over their campsite. It was triangular in shape and had rounded corners, and the man's first impression was that it was as large as a football field: hundreds of feet on a side and blotting out the sky above him.

He shouted for his friends. Meanwhile, dim, circular white lights lit at the three corners of the object and a large, prominent red light in the center of the craft began to strobe. The object began to emit a whining sound.

Could this image be a flying saucer? Or is it a hoax? With the popularity of alien life and UFOs, some people find enjoyment in creating hoaxes, either for entertainment or to gain fame through their "discovery."

Two of the campers came out in time to witness the object moving away toward a nearby mountain. They had the object in sight for almost a minute as it maneuvered up a narrow canyon in the side of the mountain. They described its motion as "like a hockey puck gliding over ice," very smooth and unwavering.

Two of the men were so unnerved that they spent the rest of the night in a motel. The men who stayed behind reported that the next morning two jet fighters flew down the same valley the object had flown up the night before, passing directly over their camp. The jets didn't move through the canyon as smoothly as the mysterious object.

This artist's rendering of an alien spacecraft hovering over the horizon could be similar to the one spotted by campers in Washington state. They did not have time to snap a picture.

Alien Elk-napping?

In the mountains of Washington state, fourteen forestry workers were planting seedling trees when three of them noticed a small, disc-shaped object drifting over a nearby ridge. At first the three thought it might be a parachute, but they quickly realized that it wasn't. It silently descended into a valley north of them with a slight "wobble" to its flight, traveling toward a herd of elk. It succeeded in getting quite close to the animals before the elk bolted. Most of them ran up a slope to their east.

One adult, however, trotted north. The object quickly moved directly above the lone elk and lifted it off the ground, though the watching men couldn't see how this was done.

The object seemed to "wobble" more. As it rose higher, the elk that was suspended below the disc rotated slowly beneath it and seemed to be pulled closer to it. The witnesses said that the object seemed to grow slightly after it had picked up the animal.

With the elk below it, the object slowly ascended the slope toward some trees. It seemed to brush the tops of the trees and then reverse its course. Making a 360-degree turn, which resulted in greater altitude, it headed toward the trees once more, moving more quickly and at a steeper angle.

As it climbed higher, the men could no longer see the elk and they assumed that it must have been brought into the craft, although they hadn't seen any sort of door through which it might have entered. The object continued to ascend and simply disappeared from sight.

CROP CIRCLES

There have been photographs of UFOs—most proven to be fakes—and the word of people claiming to have seen strange things in the sky. But many skeptics ask what hard evidence do we actually have? And in response, many believers would point to the crop circle phenomenon.

Crop circles are strange patterns created by the flattening of crops, such as wheat, barley, or rye. Sometimes the patterns are extremely elaborate, and all of them can be better viewed from above. But how did they get there?

No one knows when the first crop circle appeared. It may have been before cameras were invented or before it was even possible to fly over a field and notice a strange pattern. Many crop circles frequently appear near ancient artifacts, most famously near Stonehenge in southern England.

Experts noticed a rise in reports of crop circles in the 1900s, but was it because there were more crop circles or because people began to take notice?

There is a wealth of resources on the Internet showing interested pranksters how they can make their own crop circles using some rope and pieces of wood. But the idea had to some from someplace. Were crop circles invented by humans, or someone (or something) else?

Afterward, the witnesses said the herd of elk remained in the general area, but more closely huddled together than they had been. One of the witnesses added, "And so were we."

If their account is true, what happened to the elk if it was in fact taken aboard an alien spacecraft? Some conspiracy theorists may argue that the extraterrestrials are just trying to learn more about life on Earth by studying its strange creatures. This would not be the first example of alien abduction. And it likely won't be the last.

I f you've been living on Earth for longer than a few minutes, you've likely read a book or watched a movie or TV show inspired by the UFO phenomenon. And it's nothing new to enjoy this type of entertainment. For well over a hundred years, authors have been looking up at the sky and putting what they dream about down on paper or filming their stories from behind the camera lens.

Aliens Want to Destroy Us!

H.G. Wells published *The War of the Worlds* in 1898. In it, alien invaders came to Earth and began to destroy everything and everyone in their path, only to be stopped by their own inability to protect themselves from the microorganisms that also inhabit Earth. Some call the book the most important book in the history of science fiction, because it opened the reading public up to the idea of alien invasion.

In 1938, Orson Welles—who would go on to be one of the most famous actors and directors in the history of cinema—unwittingly took Wells's famous novel and brought it to infamy. Before television was introduced into every home, families gathered around their radios for entertainment. So on October 30, 1938, millions of people were listening when Orson Welles's popular radio program presented an adaptation of *The War of the Worlds*. But Welles wanted to do something a little bit different; he wanted the program to sound like an actual radio broadcast from start to finish. Many listeners who tuned in late and missed the introduction—the one telling them that it was all for entertainment—were quickly convinced that America was actually being attacked by aliens! There was a widespread panic, one of the worst cases of mass hysteria in American history. While the events of the original novel took place in England, the setting for Welles's broadcast moved the invasion to the small town of Grover's Mill, New Jersey. Residents of Grover's Mill and nearby Trenton leaped into action, many preparing to leave town.

The War of the Worlds has maintained its popularity over the last century. In 1996, movie audiences saw the reinvention of the story with the box office smash *Independence Day*. Rather than actual viruses, in *Independence Day* the invaders were instead thwarted by computer viruses. And 2005 brought with it Steven Spielberg's *War of the Worlds*, starring Tom Cruise and Dakota Fanning. The novel is over one hundred years old, but the very real idea of invaders from space is an idea that maintains its popularity.

If aliens do exist and have visited Earth, what do they want from humans? Are they scouting our planet for supplies? Trying to communicate? Or could it be something else?

Aliens Are Just Here for a Visit

But what if, unlike *The War of the Words*, UFOs aren't bringing extraterrestrials to Earth for malevolent purposes, but to study humans and communicate?

The 1977 film *Close Encounters of the Third Kind* asked that very question. Mysterious lights in the sky begin to appear. Roy Neary, played by Richard Dreyfuss, is one of the first to witness them. As he begins to find himself drawn to the aliens, eventually bringing him to Devil's Tower in

Science fiction writers always seem to be looking for the next completely original way of writing about UFO encounters. In the 2006 graphic novel *Cowboys & Aliens*, creator Scott Mitchell Rosenberg does just that. When a spaceship arrives in the Wild West to take over Earth, what they don't count on is a group of cowboys standing in their way. A movie based on the graphic novel, starring Daniel Craig, Harrison Ford, and Sam Rockwell, was released in 2011.

Wyoming, he soon discovers that the aliens are not there to harm humans, only to learn more about them and communicate. What begins as a terrifying encounter with mysterious lights in the sky ends with a touching first contact with beings from another planet.

Friendly extraterrestrials also appear in the films *Cocoon* and *E.T.: The Extraterrestrial* and in the animated film *Lilo & Stitch*.

CHAPTER 7

The Future of UFOs and Sightings

What should you do if you see a UFO? The same thing you should do if you witness an accident.

1. First, remain calm. If you get too excited you might forget important details.

2. Notice things. Note the time when you first see the object. When it disappears make note of what time the sighting ends. Establish what direction the object came from and where it went. Were there airplanes in the sky at the same time? If so, where were they in relation to the object and what were they doing (for example, were they chasing it)?

3. If you have a camera, take pictures. If at all possible try to include something that will give an idea of the object's size, such as a tree or telephone pole.

MOST VIDEOS ARE FAKED

Spending time on YouTube, you will likely encounter hundreds, if not thousands, of alleged videos of "sightings" of aliens and UFOs. With computer technology or the right prop or costume, almost anyone can fake a video of a sighting. How can you tell the difference between a real sighting and a clever fake?

1. Check news sites around the area of the sighting for confirmation that it was genuine. If you find nothing, it was probably fake.

2. If you find an article about the sighting or have seen the video on several Web sites, submit it to Snopes.com. The fact-finding Web site specializes in separating hoaxes and urban legends from reality.

3. Keep in mind that there are lots of sightings, and most of them are unconfirmed. It's usually best to assume that the video is fake until proved otherwise.

4. As soon as possible write down what you have seen. This is where your attention to details, such as the time and the direction of the object's flight, will come in handy. Make a diagram of the flight path, including any zigzagging it made. Make a drawing of the object itself.

5. If you are with others when the sighting occurs, do not discuss what you've seen until everyone has written about it and made his or her own drawings. Witnesses almost always see things differently, and when they discuss the event they may change each other's memory of what they've witnessed.

6. If the UFO has left physical evidence, such as pieces of metal or even footprints, do not touch them. Leave them as they are, perhaps placing a marker beside the evidence to make it easier to find again.

7. VERY IMPORTANT. Do not approach the UFO if it should land or come close to the earth. There have been reports of people suffering burns or developing strange, warty growths over their exposed skin. So don't take chances.

8. Report the sighting as soon as possible. Contact one of the following:
UFO Reporting and Information Service (206-721-5035)
Mutual UFO Network (888-817-2220)
National UFO Reporting Center (206-722-3000)

GLOSSARY

briefing paper A short statement or summary of important facts.

CB Citizens band radio.

ceiling The maximum altitude that a given aircraft can reach.

debriefing To be asked questions about a completed mission or undertaking.

debris Scattered fragments, especially of wreckage.

diagram A drawing meant to represent an object or area showing the relation between parts or places.

disk A flat, thin circular object.

dogfight Close combat between fighter aircraft.

extraterrestrial Outside the earth or its atmosphere. An alien being.

gasbag Basically a balloon, something made to hold lighter-than-air gas.

hieroglyphic Words written in the form of pictures instead of letters.

interceptor A small jet aircraft designed to catch and fight other planes.

magnitude A thing's size or extent. In astronomy, it refers to the relative brightness of a star, ranging from a rating of one for the brightest to six for those just visible to the naked eye.

maneuverable Capable of quick and light or skillful movement.

metallic Metal-like in appearance.

meteor Any particle of matter that can be observed by its heat and glow upon entering the atmosphere.

nautical mile A unit of approximately 2,025 yards (1,852 m).

reference point A fixed place from which position and distance are reckoned.

rotating When something is turning, or being caused to turn, on its axis or center.

spectrograph An apparatus for photographing the spectrum.

spectrographic analysis A spectrum is like a fingerprint, in that every material produces a unique spectrum. Spectrographic analysis provides information about an object's chemical composition.

squadron A unit of ten to eighteen aircraft.

strobe Intense, very brief flashes of light.

tower The control tower: a tall building at an airport from which air traffic is controlled.

transport A ship or aircraft used to carry soldiers or supplies.

FOR MORE INFORMATION

Center for the Study of Extraterrestrial Intelligence (CSETI)
P.O. Box 4556
Largo, MD 20775
(888) 382-7384
Web site: http://www.cseti.org
CSETI is a nonprofit international scientific organization dedicated to investigating extraterrestrial intelligence.

International UFO Museum and Research Center
114 North Main Street
Roswell, NM 88203
(800) 822-3545
Web site: http://www.roswellufomuseum.com
This museum is dedicated to the preservation of Roswell research and artifacts.

MUFON Ontario
1395 Lawrence Avenue West
Suite 20030
Toronto, ON M6L 1A7
Canada
(905) 278-9596
Web site: http://www.virtuallystrange.net/ufo/mufonontario/mufonindex.html
MUFON Ontario maintains a sighting database. It counts medical professionals and scientists amongst its membership and facilitates access to major research laboratories across Canada for UFO researchers.

Mutual UFO Network (MUFON)
2619 11th Street Road
Greeley, CO 80634
(888) 817-2220
Web site: http://www.mufon.com
This organization is dedicated to investigating UFO sightings, promoting research on UFOs, and educating the public on the UFO phenomenon.

National Aviation Reporting Center on Anomalous Phenomena
235 Louisiana Street
Vallejo, CA 94590
(707) 554-0886
Web site: http://www.narcap.org
The National Aviation Reporting Center on Anomalous Phenomena was established late in the year 2000 in response to an identified need for high quality scientific and technological data about so-called anomalous aerial phenomena of various kinds and U.S. aviation safety.

Web Sites

Due to the changing nature of Internet links, Rosen Publishing has developed an online list of Web sites related to the subject of this book. This site is updated regularly. Please use this link to access the list:

http://www.rosenlinks.com/me/ufo

Alexander, John B. *UFOs: Myths, Conspiracies, and Realities.* New York, NY: Thomas Dunne Books, 2011.

Bullard, Thomas, E. *The Myth and Mystery of UFOs.* Lawrence, KS: University Press of Kansas, 2010.

Carey, Thomas J. *Witness to Roswell: Unmasking the Government's Biggest Cover-Up.* Pompton Plains, NJ: Career Press, 2009.

Friedman, Stanton, T. *Flying Saucers and Science: A Scientist Investigates the Mysteries of UFOs.* Pompton Plains, NJ: Career Press, 2008.

Friedman, Stanton T., and Kathleen Marden. *Captured!: The Betty and Barney Hill UFO Experience.* Pompton Plains, NJ: Career Press, 2007.

Imbrogno, Philip J. *Ultraterrestrial Contact: A Paranormal Investigator's Explorations into the Hidden Abduction Epidemic.* Woodbury, MN: Llewellyn Publications, 2010.

Kean, Leslie. *UFOs: Generals, Pilots, and Government Officials Go on the Record.* New York, NY: Crown, 2010.

Marcel, Jesse. *Roswell Legacy: The Untold Story of the First Military Officer at the 1947 Crash Site.* Pompton Plains, NJ: Career Press, 2008.

Matthews, Rupert. *Roswell: Uncovering the Secrets of Area 51 and the Fatal UFO Crash.* London, England: Quercus, 2009.

Matthews, Rupert. *UFOs: A History of Alien Activity from Sightings to Abductions to Global Threat.* Secaucus, NJ: Chartwell, 2009.

Pilkington, Mark. *Mirage Men: An Adventure into Paranoia, Espionage, Psychological Warfare, and UFOs.* New York, NY: Skyhorse, 2010.

Randle, Kevin D. *Crash: When UFOs Fall from the Sky: A History of Famous Incidents, Conspiracies, and Cover-Ups.* Pompton Plains, NJ: Career Press, 2010.

Redfern, Nick. *Body Snatchers in the Desert: The Horrible Truth at the Heart of Roswell.* New York, NY: Simon & Schuster, 2005.

Redfern, Nick. *The NASA Conspiracies: The Truth Behind the Moon Landings, Censored Photos, and the Face on Mars.* Pompton Plains, NJ: New Page Books, 2010.

Vallee, Jacques. *Wonders in the Sky: Unexplained Aerial Objects from Antiquity to Modern Times.* New York, NY: Tarcher, 2010.

INDEX

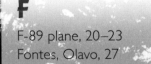

About the Authors

Dillon H. Richards is an author and UFO enthusiast who lives in Michigan.

Janet I. Stirling is an author of books for children and teens.

Photo Credits

Cover, p.1, and interior backgrounds Chip Simons/Taxi/Getty Images; cover, p. 1 (lens) © www.istockphoto.com/jsemeniuk; cover (inset), pp. 1 (inset), 6, 12, 24, 26, 28, 30–31, 34, 40, 48, 53 Shutterstock.com; p. 5 Aaron Foster/ Photographer's Choice/Getty Images; p. 7 KRT/Newscom; p. 9 © 2006 TopFoto/Fortean/The Image Works; pp. 10, 46, 54 © www.istockphoto.com/ Patrick Breig; pp. 14, 18 © Mary Evans Picture Library/The Image Works; p. 21 © AP Images; p. 22 Hemera Technologies/Photos.com/Thinkstock; p. 35 NASA/Archive Photos/Getty Images; p. 37 NASA; p. 39 MPI/Archive Photos/ Getty Images; pp. 42–43 © Lenscap/Alamy; p. 44 Victor Habbick Visions/ Science Photo Library/Getty Images; pp. 50–51 Hemera/Thinkstock.

Designer: Matt Cauli; Editor: Bethany Bryan
Photo Researcher: Peter Tomlinson